MICHAEL JACKSON

by K.C. Kelley

Consultant: Starshine Roshell
Music and Entertainment Journalist
Santa Barbara, California

New York, New York

Credits

Cover, © Pictorial Press Ltd./Alamy; 4, © Phil Dent/Redferns/Getty Images; 5, © Ron Frehm/AP Photo; 6, © Everett Collection/Shutterstock; 7, © Starstock/Photoshot/Newscom; 8, © Starstock/Photoshot/Newscom; 9, © Pictorial Press Ltd./Alamy; 10, © Granamour Weems Collection/Alamy; 11, © AH2/ZJE/WENN/Newscom; 13, © Motown Productions/Universal Pictures/Ronald Grant Archive/Alamy; 14, © AP Photo/Doug Pizac; 15, © MCA/Universal/Courtesy: Everett Collection; 16, © London Entertainment/Newscom; 17, © AP Photo/Rusty Kennedy; 18, © PA Images/Alamy; 19, © AP Photo/Joel Ryan; 20, © MJJPictures.com; 21, © ZUMA Press Inc./Alamy; 22T, © AP Photo/Doug Pizac; 22B, © Mavrixonline.com/Newscom; 23, © Splash News/Alamy.

Publisher: Kenn Goin
Creative Director: Spencer Brinker
Production and Photo Research: Shoreline Publishing Group LLC

Library of Congress Cataloging-in-Publication Data

Names: Kelley, K. C. author. | Roshell, Starshine.
Title: Michael Jackson / by K.C. Kelley ; consultant: Starshine Roshell.
Description: New York, New York : Bearport Publishing, 2019. | Series:
    Amazing Americans: Pop music stars | Includes bibliographical references
    and index.
Identifiers: LCCN 2018018013 (print) | LCCN 2018020517 (ebook) |
    ISBN 9781684027255 (ebook) | ISBN 9781684026791 (library)
Subjects: LCSH: Jackson, Michael, 1958-2009--Juvenile literature. | Rock
    musicians—United States—Biography—Juvenile literature.
Classification: LCC ML3930.J25 (ebook) | LCC ML3930.J25 K45 2018 (print) |
    DDC 782.42166092 [B]—dc23
LC record available at https://lccn.loc.gov/2018018013

Copyright © 2019 Bearport Publishing Company, Inc. All rights reserved. No part of this publication may be reproduced in whole or in part, stored in any retrieval system, or transmitted in any form or by any means, electronic, mechanical, photocopying, recording, or otherwise, without written permission from the publisher.

For more information, write to Bearport Publishing Company, Inc., 45 West 21st Street, Suite 3B, New York, New York 10010.

CONTENTS

King of Pop 4
Early Start 6
The Jackson 5 8
Little Star 10
So Many Talents! 12
Thriller 14
Star Power 16
A Sad End 18
Remembering Michael 20

Timeline 22
Glossary 23
Index 24
Read More 24
Learn More Online 24
About the Author 24

King of Pop

Fans screamed! Lights flashed! Michael Jackson twirled around and kicked up his leg. Then he glided backwards across the stage. It was 1988, and Michael was on tour. He was the most amazing performer the world had ever seen!

One of Michael's most famous dance moves is the moonwalk. To perform it, he pushed off the ground with the balls of his feet. Then, he glided backwards.

Michael on stage in Indianapolis, Indiana, in 1988

Early Start

Michael Joseph Jackson was born in Gary, Indiana, on August 29, 1958. He grew up with nine brothers and sisters. Michael's father, Joe, loved music. He encouraged Michael and his brothers to sing and dance. Joe believed his children could one day become stars.

Janet, one of Michael's sisters, is a **talented** singer.

Michael (top right) and his brothers

The Jackson 5

In 1964, Michael's dad helped five of his sons form a singing group. It was called The Jackson 5. In 1969, the family moved to Los Angeles. The Jackson 5 made their first record there. It soon became a smash hit!

Michael was the lead singer of the group's hit songs, "ABC" and "I'll Be There."

Little Star

Little Michael stood out from his brothers. His high, clear voice and dance moves thrilled young fans. In 1972, Michael started making his own music. "Rockin' Robin" and "Got to Be There" were his first hit songs.

Michael and The Jackson 5 performed on popular TV shows, such as *The Ed Sullivan Show*.

Ed Sullivan and little Michael

Michael performing by himself in 1974

So Many Talents!

In 1978, Michael tried something new. He starred in a movie called *The Wiz*. The movie was based on the famous Wizard of Oz books. Michael's performance wowed viewers. The next year, Michael released his **solo** album, *Off the Wall*. Fans loved it. Michael had become one of the biggest stars in the world!

With *Off the Wall*, Michael became the first solo artist with four Billboard Top 10 singles.

Michael (bottom) played the Scarecrow in *The Wiz*.

Thriller

In 1982, Michael's fame grew. His album *Thriller* was a huge hit and sold millions of copies. For the title song, he made a groundbreaking music video. A year later, *Thriller* became the best-selling album of all time! It is still number one today.

Thriller won eight **Grammys**, including Album of the Year.

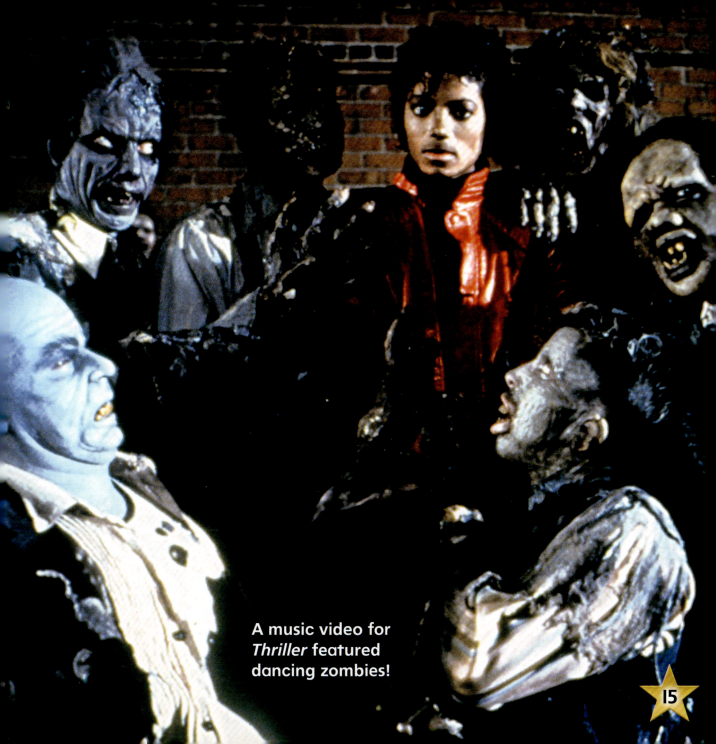

A music video for *Thriller* featured dancing zombies!

Star Power

In 1992, Michael revealed he had a skin disorder called vitiligo (vit-uhl-EYE-goh). It was the first of many **medical** issues for Michael. Still, he kept performing. At the Super Bowl in 1993, he put on a fantastic halftime show.

Michael also had several **operations** on his nose.

Michael performing at Super Bowl XXVII (27) in Pasadena, California

A Sad End

Michael struggled with health issues through the early 2000s. He was also having money problems. Michael planned a new tour called *This Is It*. It sold millions of tickets. He was set for a big **comeback**. Then, Michael died suddenly on June 25, 2009. Fans around the world were stunned.

Michael had three children—Prince, Blanket, and Paris.

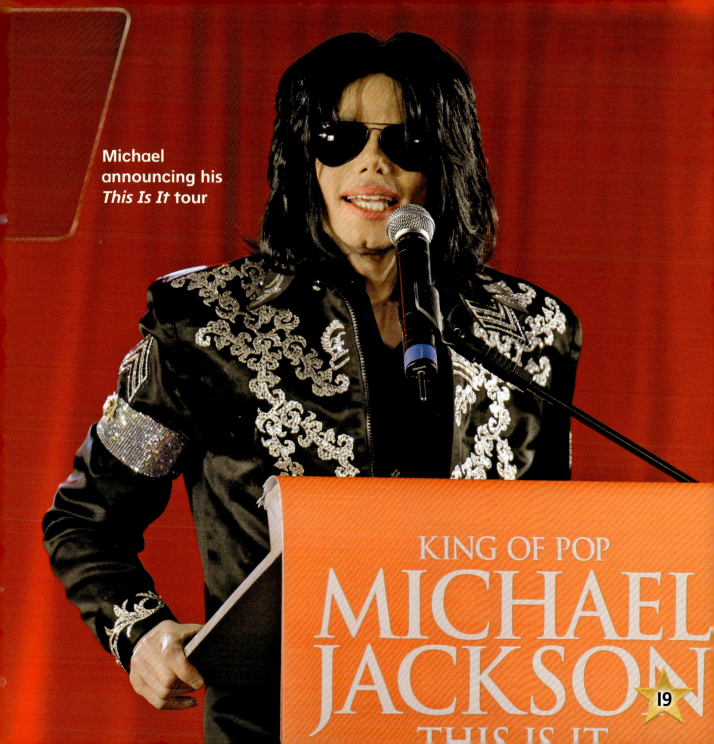

Michael announcing his *This Is It* tour

Remembering Michael

Michael remains one of the greatest pop stars of all time. Millions of people still love his music. A show in Las Vegas called *One* was created to **honor** him. Though his life ended too soon, Michael Jackson's amazing music will live on forever.

In 2006, *Guinness World Records* named Michael the Most Successful Entertainer of All Time.

Michael with his pet chimpanzees

Timeline

Here are some key dates in Michael Jackson's life.

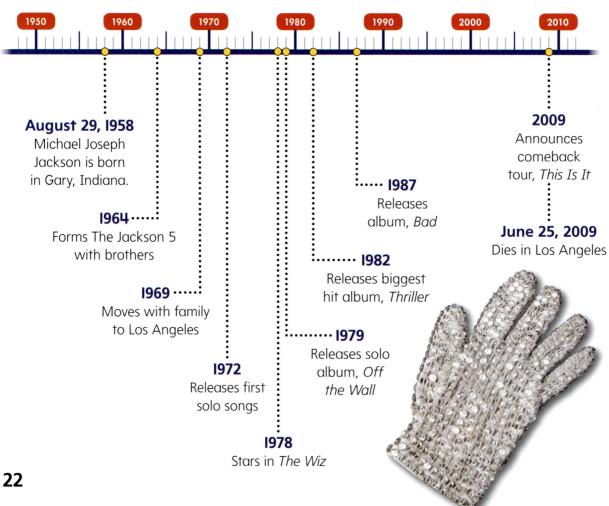

August 29, 1958
Michael Joseph Jackson is born in Gary, Indiana.

1964
Forms The Jackson 5 with brothers

1969
Moves with family to Los Angeles

1972
Releases first solo songs

1978
Stars in *The Wiz*

1979
Releases solo album, *Off the Wall*

1982
Releases biggest hit album, *Thriller*

1987
Releases album, *Bad*

2009
Announces comeback tour, *This Is It*

June 25, 2009
Dies in Los Angeles

Glossary

comeback (KUM-bak) a return to something after being away for a while

Grammys (GRAM-eez) awards given each year to the top musicians

honor (ON-ur) to give praise or an award to someone

medical (MED-uh-kuhl) having to do with medicine and doctors

operations (op-uh-RAY-shuns) procedures to repair or improve the body

solo (SOH-loh) done by one person

talented (TAL-uhn-tid) having the ability to do something very well

Index

brothers 6–7, 8–9, 10
family 6–7, 8–9, 10, 18
Grammys 14
Guinness World Records 20
Jackson, Janet 6
Jackson, Joe 6, 8
Jackson 5, The 8–9, 10, 22
moonwalk 4
Off the Wall 12, 22
One 20
Sullivan, Ed 10
Super Bowl XXVII 16–17
This Is It tour 18–19, 22
Thriller 14–15, 22
vitiligo 16
Wiz, The 12–13, 22

Read More

Stine, Megan. *Who Was Michael Jackson?* New York: Grosset & Dunlap (2015).

Tieck, Sarah. *Michael Jackson: Music Legend (Big Buddy Biographies).* Edina, MN: ABDO (2011).

Learn More Online

To learn more about Michael Jackson, visit
www.bearportpublishing.com/AmazingAmericans

About the Author

K.C. Kelley has written more than 200 books for young readers, including many biographies. His favorite Michael Jackson song is "Man in the Mirror."